401 CONFIDENTIAL

How 401(k) companies get FAT on your money... while you slave at your cubicle.

Brought To You By

ORLANDO
401k Specialists

Michael J. Marini

President / Financial Adviser

ISBN-10: 1717219500

ISBN-13: 978-1717219503

401 CONFIDENTIAL

How 401(k) companies get FAT on your money...
while you slave at your cubicle.

Michael J. Marini

Foreword

It happens right under your nose. The Department of Labor requires them to disclose to employer and employee how much they take out of your retirement account and what it pays for. But it doesn't matter. You trust them. Your employer trusts them. You heard the fees are good. And truthfully, you wouldn't know if the fees are good or not. It's not what you do. They do what they do. You do what you do. That's what they count on.

But here's the thing. You don't see it. According to 401ksource.com, you could be losing 4% or more of your retirement dollars to fees and you and your employer be completely unaware. Your money is long gone by the time you pull out your smartphone to check your balance, and they don't even leave you a note. And do not think for one second that you are immune because you work for a large employer or because your plan is stocked with low-cost mutual funds. Low-cost mutual funds are not the culprit. They are the diversion. These retirement plan companies are smarter than you. They are smarter than your employer. And they are counting on you keeping it that way.

Why did I write this book? To be your man on the inside. Have you heard the expression "you don't know what you don't know?" By showing you what you don't know, perhaps I'll have the good fortune of meeting you and we'll end up working together. I serve individual clients, small businesses, large corporations and local and state governments with retirement plans, investments, life insurance, disability insurance and ACA & ERISA compliance services.

I also thought it would be cool to save people a billion dollars a year in retirement plan fees. This book can do way more that, but I should probably keep my expectations realistic.

Each chapter of this book is written to build your knowledge from the ground up. I take complicated topics and speak about them in ways that third-graders can master by recess. The simplicity is what makes it powerful for you. If you are an employer frustrated with your retirement plan, you've come to the right place. If you are an extremely plugged-in 401(k) participant concerned about fees, you've come to the right place. If you think 401(kay) is pronounced 401(kuh), you've come to the right place. This book will enrich you and make your life better. Each chapter will teach you something new and your future will be brighter for it.

Whether you are the 401(k) decision-maker at your company, plan participant, wondering if you should join your plan, or even if your company doesn't have a retirement plan, this is the book for you. You might just be the one to share this book with your company and get a retirement plan started. Or you might just be the hero who shows your organization how to save everyone hundreds of thousands of dollars by switching to a lower-cost plan.

Ask any employer or employee who has been through the retirement plan wars and they will tell you. The best 401(k), 403(b) and 457(b) plans come about when employees speak their concerns, and everyone pulls together to make your organization's retirement plan the best it can be.

I created a section at the back of the book for making notes and calculating fees as you dig through your plan's documents.

Thank you for buying this book.

Please leave a review on Amazon.

Please reach out to me if you need help.

Michael J. Marini

Email - mmarini@ksifa.com

Phone - 407 924-7950

LinkedIn - www.linkedin.com/in/michaeljmarini

Website - www.orlando401kspecialists.com

Contents

What Is a 401(k) Plan?

A 401(k) plan is a piggy bank for grown-ups that you fill up with money from your paycheck. You need a piggy bank. Everyone needs a piggy bank. Why? Did you have a piggy bank when you were a child? Think back to that time and what that piggy bank meant to you. First, it was yours and you were proud of it. Am I right? Second, it was cool. You kept it in a special place and you really enjoyed dropping those coins in and seeing how heavy it became as time went by. Third, the piggy bank wasn't something you started doing and stopped doing. You just didn't see it that way. Your piggy bank was a part of you, and I'm sure many of you reading this still have your piggy bank. Others reading this probably wish you knew what happened to yours, myself included. Mine was chrome and I can still see that smiling piggy's face.

Now if the notion of a grown-up piggy bank sounds a little silly to you, ask yourself this. What do wealthy people have that most people only wish they had? Piggy banks. Really fat piggy banks.

I could go on all day espousing reasons why you should be in a retirement plan and why you should pay attention to fees, but those would be my reasons. You have your own reasons for doing what you do. I am not fond of reasons. I am fond of emotions because emotions are at the core of all our decisions in life. And emotionally-speaking I don't think anyone can argue the fact that piggy banks are flat-out cool, and quite frankly adorable.

If you are the kind of person who nods off when someone starts talking about retirement or investing or saving, don't think about it. Just do it. Go get your grown-up piggy bank and start stuffing it full every payday. The best time to start is immediately, and the right amount to put in is more than you think you can spare. Go big! Just like the piggy bank of your childhood you will enjoy dropping money in. You will enjoy the feeling of accomplishment as it grows heavier over time. And after finishing this book you will not see your grown-up piggy bank as something you start and stop. It will be a part of you and with you your entire life.

Now if that wasn't motivation enough, let me tell you the greatest things of all about your grown-up piggy bank. Your grown-up piggy bank does way more than just hold your money. It gives you cash back each time you drop money in. And then it turns your money into more money if you treat it right. And when you grow older and find yourself needing a helping hand in life, it stops taking money from you altogether and starts giving money back to you. Lots of it. Like clockwork. And it never stops giving back if you treat it right. Truthfully, your grown-up piggy bank loves to give way more than it loves to receive. And that is about as cool as it gets.

Where Do You Get Piggy?

You get your piggy bank at work. 401(k)s are the retirement plan of private-sector employers and are synonymous with the 403(b) and 457(b) plans of public-sector, non-profit and religious employers. The number & letter designation for each plan refers to IRS code. You can read the code for each plan by visiting www.irs.gov and typing 401k, 403b or 457b in the search bar. This is the number one place I recommend you go online to educate yourself about retirement plans and their features. I have also included helpful information and links later in "Additional Resources."

All three types of plans function the same for participants and remarkably so do the costs. The egregiousness of the fees charged by most 403(b) and 457(b) plan providers, just like their 401(k) counterparts, is nothing short of jaw-dropping. For the purposes of this book, consider the information herein to apply equally to private-sector and public-sector retirement plans. If you work in the public-sector and think you are immune to egregious fees because your 457(b) is by the well-known life insurance company that has the largest share of the business, think again. School teachers with their 403(b) TSA accounts are another extremely fee-gouged group of retirement savers. Stay with me because I am going to show you exactly how they do it.

While retirement plans are standard-fare with public-sector employers, there is no guarantee your employer in the private-sector has one. How do you find out? Just ask if they have a 401(k) plan. If it's a yes, then ask how long before you can join. Most companies will require you to be employed one year and work 1,000 hours per year to be eligible to participate. This equates to an average 20-hour workweek. If your employer does not have a 401(k) plan, ask them if they plan to offer one in the future. Some companies simply choose not to sponsor a plan, and other simply have not contemplated it. Like most employer benefits there is a cost to the business. The average fee to establish a 401(k) plan is about $500 and the annual cost of administration hovers around $1,500 per year depending on number of employees. If you are self-employed and reading this, there are several options of low-cost retirement plans available to you with no establishment fees or annual administration fees.

A common misconception in the workplace is that your employer gets something from you by you joining their plan. Nothing could be further from the truth. 401(k) plans are an employee benefit provided at a cost to employers. They gain nothing from you by sponsoring a 401(k) plan, except for a ton of responsibility and some bills. Employers typically sponsor a plan so the owners can fund their own retirement, enhance their ability to attract good employees and many are genuinely concerned about the long-term welfare of their people. Pay no attention to the 401(k) opinions of others in the workplace or online. A retirement plan is always a good thing and it is always in your best interest to participate. Getting a well-designed, low-cost plan... Well, that's another story.

Once you join a plan and get your piggy bank, the most exciting news is that you can take it with you wherever you go for the rest of your life. By the way, never cash it in. Always keep the money in there. If you leave that job for another, open a new piggy bank at the new job and transfer the piggy bank from the first employer into the second. This is called a 401(k) trustee-to-trustee transfer. If your next employer does not have a 401(k) plan, transfer your piggy bank into a personal piggy bank known as an Individual Retirement Account, or IRA. This is called a "401(k) Rollover to an IRA," or "IRA Rollover." You can add money to your IRA every pay period and receive the same benefit as you would had you access to a 401(k) plan. Another idea is to ask your employer to establish a payroll-deduction IRA plan. This is a plan whereby your employer can withhold your IRA contributions from your paycheck and place the money in your IRA account for you. It functions almost identically to a 401(k) plan, except with zero cost to the business. In fact, the only perceptible difference is in the amount you may contribute. 401(k) plans just have much higher contribution limits. This brings me to my "ABC" principle of saving money. "Always Be Contributing" to a 401(k) plan, or an Individual Retirement Account or both.

Individual Retirement Accounts, just like 401(k)s, should remain with you for life. You can even transfer your IRA into the next 401(k) plan you join. Most 401(k) plans will allow for this, although you will need to check with the plan to be sure. There is a document to every company's 401(k) plan called a Summary Plan Description, or SPD, that is available to be provided to you. If you do not have your employer's SPD, ask them for it and keep it handy. They can usually be downloaded in .pdf format. The Summary Plan Description is the bible for your 401(k) plan. It contains chapter and verse about how your company's plan is designed and how to manage your account.

No two 401(k) plans are the same. Keep a copy of your SPD for each company where you have a 401(k) plan balance. Always know what is going on with your money and never forget where you have money. Create a folder in the cloud called 401(k) and stash every IRA and 401(k) statement and SPD you receive throughout your working life. A shocking number of people leave jobs and completely forget about the money they had in their 401(k) plan.

Whether you end up with several piggy banks along your life's journey or combine them as you go along, there are three things you should always commit to doing. Always Be Contributing to a 401(k), Individual Retirement Account or both. Keep a file in the cloud so you never lose track of where you have money. And never cash out! Why never cash out? More on that later.

And lastly, don't be cynical. If you work for an employer that does not provide some of their own dollars to match your dollars that you put into your retirement plan, does that means you shouldn't participate? Hardly! But I do understand why you might feel that way. You probably listen to my favorite radio station W.I.I.F.M. What's In It For Me? Well, there's plenty in it for you even if your employer doesn't match. I will explain in the next chapter.

What's In It For You?

That is a very good question, and one that I feel is never properly addressed. One reason I believe people do not participate in 401(k) plans or achieve a great result is that nobody shows you the end game. There are too many unanswered questions like "Why should I do this?" "How much should I save?" "How does it work when I retire?" "What if I run out of money?" "Why should I even care?" If you knew more about the end game, then perhaps you might be a little more inclined to participate in a 401(k) plan and get a better result. Am I right?

How would you feel if you could receive a lifetime of monthly income starting around age 60? For as long as you live, no matter how long you live, money will just show up in your bank account each month like clockwork. Does that sound good? This is what is possible with your piggy bank. You will not only get monthly income to live on, but you will keep piggy bank nice and fat as you grow older. Your piggy bank becomes what I like to call "the big pile of money." When you have a big pile of money you get to live off the money it earns. And you also gain financial security and the peace of mind that you can handle any expense life throws your way. That's because Piggy Bank can write a check when "life happens."

This is the 401(k) end game that no one told you about. This is what's in it for you. This is why you need a piggy bank.

How much income will you get each month? It depends.
Everyone who has a 401(k), 403(b) or 457(b) plan can turn their piggy
bank into a stream of perpetual income starting around age 60 if they
know how to do it. The details of how it works and how much you will
get are better suited for a one-on-one conversation with me. But here is
what everyone needs to know to know. Step one. Get a piggy bank.
Step two. Fatten it up. The fatter your piggy bank, the larger your
monthly income can become starting around age 60. That's the whole
game. So, if you're wondering how much the right amount is to save
each payday, stop wondering. Go big!

Now, perhaps you are the kind of person who doesn't give two
cents about the notion of planning for the future. If so, I completely get
it. But if you are going to grow old anyway, why not be old in style?
Who couldn't stand some money just showing up in your bank account
every month? Not only is that cool but trust me you are going to wish
you have that when you get there. Nobody gets to age 60 and says
"Wow, I'm so glad to be broke." If you don't believe me, go find some
broke people that were born around 1960 or earlier and ask them how
they like it.

And on a final note. Would it be alright if I take a moment to
apologize on behalf of my myself and financial advisers everywhere if
we accidentally made 401(k)s and retirement planning too complicated
or boring in the past? If we put you to sleep or left you in the dust

while we were trying to sound smart, can we please just circle back and start over? O.K? Great! Thank you. Here we go.

Some retirement savings is better than no savings.

More savings is better than less savings.

Getting monthly income for retirement is good.

Not getting monthly income is not good.

Save as much as you can, as often as you can.

The earlier you start the better.

Don't forget to live for today.

Tomorrow will take care of itself.

Take time to smell the roses.

Hug the ones you love.

Pay attention to the fees.

Can we all just agree to agree? I promise on behalf of my colleagues in the investment industry that we will only speak about money in simple and meaningful ways from now on.

The Elephant In The Room

Now I know what some of you are thinking. Elephant better not step on Piggy! But seriously, who wants to wait until they are 60 to enjoy life, right? How about receiving some benefits now? Well, we have a plan for that. What if every time you dropped money in your piggy bank you could get some money back to spend now? Kind of like the points you get when you shop at your favorite store or eat at your favorite restaurant. I think the 401(k) plan was the inventor of the points system, although nobody realized it at the time. I just realized it myself as I was writing. My wife is quite into the collecting of points, which got me thinking about how the cash you get back works on the same principle as shopping rewards points.

Here is what that looks like. Every time you put money into your retirement plan the IRS gives you three ways to get money back. First, you can get cash back this year. Second, you can forgo the cash back this year and pick up the cash later around age 60 when you start getting your monthly deposits into your bank account. Lastly you can do both by putting part of your money toward the first option and part toward the second option.

If you wish to take your tax-deduction and get cash back now, this is called a "Traditional 401(k) Contribution." This is the most popular choice among savers, and the default choice in 401(k) plans. Here's how it works. The money you put in your 401(k) is deducted from Box 1 on your W-2 (Wages, tips and other compensation.) For this reason, Box 1 will be smaller than Box 3 (Social security wages.) The reason it matters is that Box 1 is the one that dictates how much you pay in federal income tax when you file.

Now here is where it gets interesting. You can put $18,500 in your 401(k) piggy bank for tax year 2018, and if you are age 50 and over you can put in $24,500. First, by participating in your plan it is conceivable that your contributions could drop you into a lower tax bracket. Should that happen you will get even MORE cash back than the amount I am about to show you. You may even consider researching your numbers to see if it could happen for you, but I don't recommend it. You should always save as much money as you can. If you drop a tax bracket by doing so, consider it your good fortune.

A quick word... Before I show you this please understand I am just using these numbers for the sake of example. Yes, this example would indicate a highly-compensated individual. But the principles work the same for everyone whether you earn a lot or a modest sum.

For the sake of illustration, I am going to say that your taxable income for tax year 2018 is $110,000 and you are a single filer.

If you contributed the maximum $18,500 to your 401(k) you will have reduced your taxable income to $91,500. Now we will look at your before and after income tax results.

Your income taxes before your 401(k) contributions are $20,689.50.

Your income taxes after your 401(k) contributions are $16,249.50

Your TAX SAVINGS are $4,440.00

Your piggy bank just gave you $4,440 all because you showed it a little love. Do you remember where I said in "What Is a 401(k) Plan" that your piggy bank gives you cash back each time you put money in? There it is! But guess what. We are not done.

Now I am going to put on my financial adviser hat and ask you a question.

How much return did you achieve in your 401(k) account just by participating? Wait a minute, you say. What could I be talking about? You have $18,500 in your 401(k) account, right? But how much did you put in your account? That's easy. $18,500. Right? Yes, but technically you put just $14,060 in your account. Remember, your piggy bank gave you back $4,440 REAL money just for participating in your retirement plan, yet your account still says $18,500.

So, what really happened here? You got your cake and you got to eat it too. The difference between *what you put in* and *what you have* is the equivalent of achieving a 31.6% return in your 401(k) account. How did I figure that? I asked myself how much growth it would take for $14,060 to become $18,500. The answer is arrived at by dividing the amount of growth ($4,440) by the principal investment ($14,060), which looks like this. ($4,440 / $14,060) = 31.6%. *This is a hypothetical example used for illustrative purposes only.*

This demonstrates a core principal of 401(k) wealth-building called "Rate of Return" which we will discuss later. But for now, let's take the win and celebrate our friend Piggy. I don't know about you, but if you ask me Piggy Bank rocks!

Now, let's look at the other option, called "Roth 401(k) Contribution." As I mentioned you can do this as a standalone option, or you can split your money each pay period between a Traditional contribution and Roth contribution.

The Roth contribution essentially flips the script on taxes. You don't get any love now in the form of cash back on your taxes. But don't worry. Piggy Bank will love you later, because you will not pay any income tax on that money when you start getting monthly deposits in your bank account around age 60. Since you decided to pay your income tax now, you will get both the money you put in and the growth on that money to spend in your retirement years with no taxes due.

The Roth Contribution is no less desirable and no less beneficial than a Traditional Contribution. It is simply different. Some people like the Traditional, some like the Roth and some like a combination of the two. What is the best way to go? This is more of a feel thing than a numbers thing.

If you are undecided but like the idea of both, then do both. I find that when it comes to paying taxes it is hard to predict the future and what will be best for you then. Therefore, don't go crazy trying to analyze taxes to the point of inaction. The only wrong action in this case is inaction. Fill that piggy bank up!

Michael J. Marini

The 401(k) Journey To Wealth

We have covered a lot of ground so far about the what, why, how and what's in it for you regarding retirement plans. Now it's time to wade a little deeper in and talk about the journey. The beautiful thing to me about 401(k) plans is that they do something magical. They give anyone from any walk of life a vehicle to create wealth and financial independence. But unfortunately, there is also an ugliness to the entire scene.

To understand why I feel this way we need to address some hard facts. Financial literacy is at an all-time low among adults in the workplace. A staggering number of businesses do not offer a 401(k) plan. A staggering number of businesses are being unwittingly fee-gouged by their 401(k) provider. A staggering number of people who have a 401(k) plan at work have simply said "no thanks." And lastly, the percentage of people who are living out a successful 401(k) end game is pathetic. We can do better, and I hope this book plays some small part in that process for you.

The reason I feel that 401(k) plans are magical is that they deliver Wall Street to Main Street. On Main Street, where most people are born and live, there is a place called the bank. The bank is the financial institution where most Americans have a level of familiarity and are accustomed to saving money. For almost everyone on Main Street the bank is the only financial institution they will ever have in their lives. Over on Wall Street lives a much smaller group of people. These people laugh off the bank, instead saving their money in stocks and bonds because they get a better return. The people who come from Main Street rarely make it over to Wall Street, and if they do they don't stay long because the place holds no charm for them.

Enter the 401(k) plan. The 401(k) plan gives anyone from any walk of life an express trip to Wall Street where they are escorted straight into the offices of companies who can help change the financial trajectory of their life. You do not need to know anyone. You do not need to read any books. You do not need to take any classes. All you have to do is walk into work tomorrow and tell your employer "I'm in." You will be welcomed with open arms and handed a set of instructions and your Wall Street trip itinerary. Now, I'm not going to say that it will all make perfect sense. The truth is that you might even end up with more questions than answers. But don't worry. Keep reading and I will get you through it.

The 401(k) Journey To Wealth is a formula by me that has five components. The good news is that three of them are provided by you and are "no-brainers." They literally require you to train yourself and then set it and forget it. The fourth component is also provided by you, via collaboration with others in your workplace after reading this book. The last component is provided by your 401(k) plan, 403(b) or 457(b) plan after you get your fees down.

Here are the five components:

1. Time

2. Money

3. Consistency

4. Low Fees

5. Rate of Return

Time is something that we have simply to define. The time you will have a piggy bank and be an investor is hereby the entire time of your life. There is no starting and stopping of the process. When you're in, you're in. There is no "in today, out tomorrow" because of something that happened or something you heard. How do I know this? I guide people throughout their working years and throughout a successful 401(k) end game. It's what I do.

Your finances can be just like your healthcare and the law. It is wise to seek the counsel of healthcare professionals and lawyers because they know more than you. Finances are the same and sometimes you need help letting go of your worst instincts. I know it is not easy because money is the most personal thing we possess in life. I am the first person to tell my clients that their money is their money and they are the boss. But if you want to do this right and you want the advice of a counselor, just know that that the Time component is defined as the entire time of your life. And do not worry. Being "In" does not mean being risky. It simply means being "In" appropriately.

Money is the money you will take from your paycheck every payday of your entire working life and put in your piggy bank. I do not care if it is just $10. You will do it and you will never stop doing it until the day you stop working and start your 401(k) end game. There are no excuses. If you think money is tight and you can't spare $10 you are missing the big picture. Never forget how Piggy Bank loves you back every time you put money in. How much money is enough? When your employer says "STOP, you are maxed out for the year." That's when you've put in enough. Here is an incentive to keep you energized. The fatter you make Piggy Bank and the sooner in life you do it, the more Piggy Bank can give you back each month in your 401(k) end game. But you already knew that.

Consistency is doing the best thing all the time. When you are working you want to be "ABC." That's "Always Be Contributing" to your 401(k), 403(b) or 457(b), or an Individual Retirement Account or both. Consistency also means never cashing out if you are between jobs or money is tight. And it also means never tinkering with your investment strategy inside your account because of some event. When you look at the arc of your entire working life and retired years, do you think that one single day out of 20,000 plus days should cause you to change a stated course of action? That is an absolute no. In fact, whether current events are good or bad you will have already factored them in. Course consistency and purposefulness should always rule the day when locked in a battle with your emotions.

Low Fees are the spark that ignites jet fuel in your retirement account. High fees are the opposite. They smother your account to the point that it smolders. There are a lot of smoldering fires across the country in private and public-sector retirement plans and I will do my best to help you re-ignite the flames.

Just to be clear on how fees work. If you have $100,000 in your account and the fees of your plan are 2%, every year they take $2,000 from your account and give it to themselves. Remember what I said at the outset. You don't see it coming out. It is long gone by the time you log in to your account. As far as you can tell everything looks normal.

Now, if you move your plan to a company where the fee is 1%, the new company takes $1,000 and you get to keep the other $1,000 in your account. What is the difference between $2,000 and $1,000? A little bit of time and effort on your part to make a change. What happens if you don't do anything? Well, by the time your account reaches $200,000 you'll be giving them $4,000. And when you reach $300,000 you'll be giving them $6,000. The price tag for doing nothing goes up every year. And believe me, your expensive plan provider loves this about you. They especially love when they talk circles around you and convince you are already receiving discounts and fee concessions because of how much they value their relationship with you.

In every company and governmental agency there exists a decision-maker or a committee of people who make the retirement plan vendor decision. But even these people don't know what is going on right in front of them. Lawmakers for years have known this and tried to solve this problem. They have been mostly unsuccessful because they exist outside the veil. Try as they may to legislate your attention, there is a trust veil that exists between employer and retirement plan vendor where decisions get made. Fee structures are purposefully complicated. The system is designed to work against you. And as I said earlier. "You wouldn't know if the fees are good or not. It's not what you do. They do what they do. You do what you do. That's what they count on."

Retirement plan providers exist only because of the dollars coming out of your paycheck. The ones that are fee-gouging your retirement plan balances are getting away with it because you let them. You have the power. Take away the dollars. It is that simple. No company that is fee-gouging is going to call you up and offer you a voluntary fee reduction. Why would they? You are in the dark and they already have your business. They think of you every two weeks when you put money in your account and they smile.

Retirement plan companies are greedy. And they are not unwise to the notion that you don't like being fee-gouged. They are prepared for you and have one job when you come calling about "the fees." That job is to intimidate you to the point of inaction, so your business stays on their books. You may be in for a fight if you try to talk sense with them. Meet them head-on with numbers and do not let them spin. Quite frankly, if you are in this situation the best thing to do is just get out. Do not waste your time even having the conversation. The reason will come clear to you when you learn about Rate of Return. There is a finite amount of your money to go around and you simply cannot afford to give it away.

Rate of Return is the mathematical engine that powers the growth of your money inside your 401(k) plan. You cannot accumulate the amount of money you need for a successful 401(k) end game with simply the money you put in. That money needs to grow. Once you understand Rate of Return and its relationship to fees things will click for you. I believe you will want to do all you can to ensure that you pay only low fees.

Let's take a trip through town...

Over on Main Street at the First National Bank, people typically earn about 1% per year in their savings account. How good is that? Well, at a 1% rate of return their money will double itself about every 72 years. For example, if you put $10 from the tooth fairy in when you're six and never touch it, you'll have $20 when you're 78. If you live to be 150 years old your money will double itself again to $40. This is called "compound interest."

If you are trying to set yourself up to get lifetime income from your 401(k) around age 60, how successful will you be if you save at the bank on Main Street? Obviously, you won't. You'll have barely more money than the money you put in. Thankfully, your 401(k) is your express ticket to Wall Street. Hop in because we are moving.

Over on Wall Street people invest in stocks and bonds because they produce much higher returns over this same long period of your life. Stocks and bonds just happen to be the investments offered inside your 401(k) plan. Each time you put money in you are purchasing shares of stocks and bonds that are pre-selected and pooled together to make it easy for you to invest. You do not need any special knowledge to do this successfully. You need only to focus on my first three components of Time, Money and Consistency.

So how do Wall Street's higher returns help you? Let's say for example that you start earning 4% returns instead of 1%. Your money will now double itself four times over that same 72-year period. If you started out with the same $10, it would become $20 by age 24, then $40 by age 42, then $80 by age 60 and $160 by the time you reached age 78. The difference between 1% and 4% is the difference between $20 and $160 after 72 years of your life.

At 4% we are doing better, but we are not even close to you achieving a successful 401(k) end game. You are still not earning enough growth to reach your goal. Let's go ahead and double that 4% rate of return to 8%. Keep in mind, if you achieved 8% it would be the average of returns over your lifetime. Some years you could earn less when investing in stocks and bonds. Some years you could earn more. Some years you could even see a decline in your account. Do not worry. In fact, rest easy. You automatically turn this into your advantage when you follow my principles of Time, Money and Consistency.

Hold on because at 8% we are picking up speed. We are now going to shorten the doubling period for our money to 9 years. This will enable us to compound our $10 from the tooth fairy eight times over the same 72-year period. Our original $10 saving would become:

1. $20 by age 15

2. $40 by age 24

3. $80 by age 33

4. $160 by age 42

5. $320 by age 51

6. $640 by age 60

7. $1,280 by age 69

8. $2,560 by age 78.

As you can see, the difference between 1% and 8% returns over 72 years of your life is the difference between $20 and $2,560.

This is Rate of Return. It is critical to you achieving a successful 401(k) end game. You should do everything in your power to achieve Rate of Return, and then work just as hard to avoid giving it away to fee-gouging retirement plan companies. What good is it if you bust your butt to earn 8% and your plan provider chops off 3% or 4% for themselves? Are they looking out for you? They are looking out for them. That means something needs to happen. And it starts with you going on a no-holds barred search for the truth about your plan's fees.

Michael J. Marini

The Chilling Impact Of Fees

Now that we understand of how Rate of Return impacts investment growth, let's look at a more precise example and how it affects you.

Remember, 401(k) fees have already been deducted from your 401(k) balance by the time you pull out your smartphone. Your chances of understanding how fees are impacting your bottom line by simply looking at your account are virtually zero. It will take a much deeper dive to get to the bottom of things.

This is a hypothetical example of a person who joins a 401(k) plan at age 21 and saves $4,992 per year until age 60. The payroll is bi-weekly and the contributions are $192. The rate of return is 8% annually, net of 401(k) plan fees.

Results Summary	
Initial deposit amount	$0.00
Start date	2/11/2018
End date	3/11/2057
Dates span a period of	39 years 1 month 1 day
Periodic deposit (withdrawal)	$192.00 Bi-weekly, at the end of each period.
Rate of return	8% compounded annually
Number of deposits (withdrawals)	1,019
Total deposits (withdrawals)	$195,648.00
Future value of initial deposit	$0.00
Future value of periodic deposits	$1,251,880.16
Calculated future value	$1,251,880.16 as of 3/11/2057

Now let's look at our hypothetical person's twin who took a job just up the street. They too are saving $192 every two weeks. However, their plan's fees are 2% higher and they are netting just a 6% return in their 401(k) plan.

Results Summary	
Initial deposit amount	$0.00
Start date	2/11/2018
End date	3/11/2057
Dates span a period of	39 years 1 month 1 day
Periodic deposit (withdrawal)	$192.00 Bi-weekly, at the end of each period.
Rate of return	6% compounded annually
Number of deposits (withdrawals)	1,019
Total deposits (withdrawals)	$195,648.00
Future value of initial deposit	$0.00
Future value of periodic deposits	$751,828.74
Calculated future value	$751,828.74 as of 3/11/2057

One of the twins reaches age 60 with $1,251,880. The other reaches age 60 with just $751,828. That is half a million dollars less! They both did everything the same, but one got steamrolled by high 401(k) fees. Is that fair?

If this were happening to you right now, wouldn't you want to know so you could do something about it? I estimate that this is happening to 90 out of 100 people in the workplace right now. This includes both the private and the public sector. It may not be as bad as 2% for you, but there is a high probability that you are not among the

Michael J. Marini

approximately 10% that are paying only low or reasonably low 401(k), 403(b) or 457(b) fees.

Knowing how vital Rate of Return is to your ability to grow your money and achieve a successful 401(k) end game, how much of your returns are you willing to needlessly give away?

Knowing that time is your most precious resource, and that your doubling periods for your money grow longer with every 1% in fees you give away, how much fee-gouging are you willing to settle for?

Understanding that your goal is to achieve as much growth as you can by age 60, do you think it wise to give away 1% of your money each year to fee-gouging? How about 1.5%? How about 2%?

Everything about your 401(k) journey is finite. The amount of money you can save is finite. The returns you can earn in your investments are finite. The number of years you can work and save for your 401(k) end game are finite. Do you think it wise to remain indifferent if money is pouring out of the bottom of your account unnoticed and unchecked?

Let's work together and check it. If we find a hole, let's get that hole plugged!

Dirty Little Secrets

These are all the ways retirement plan companies get FAT on your money while you slave at your cubicle.

Dirty Little Secret #1 - The Separate Account Charge

I made this #1 because it costs Americans more than $1 billion every year. This charge is found exclusively in retirement plans sold by life insurance companies. The average charge in the plans I have examined is a gut-punching 1.25%. The charge in the plan illustrated next chapter in "Let's Tackle The Fees" is a whopping 1.85%.

If your 401(k), 403(b) or 457(b) plan is by a life insurance company, you are forced to pay this insidious fee. Get a retirement plan that is not by a life insurance company and you won't have to. It is that simple. These plans are also often stocked with high-cost investments.

Look for the signs:

1. Your retirement plan is by a life insurance company.

2. Look for keywords *Group Variable Annuity, Separate Account Charge, Variable Account Charge, Mortality & Expense Charge.*

3. Your statements value your investments in "units," not "shares."

If your organization has this crushing brand of 401(k), 403(b) or 457(b) plan, you can get rid of the high fees by ditching the life insurance company and moving your plan to a 401(k) advisory firm.

Many fee-enlightened employers in both the private and public-sector have made the move and never looked back.

Dirty Little Secret #2 - Pricing Thresholds

401(k) providers often charge smaller businesses higher fees and reward them with fee reductions if their plan assets surpass pricing thresholds. They will tell you that they incur larger costs to service smaller plans. It is simply not true. Taking you on as a client did not cause them to hire additional staff. Nor did it cause them to expend additional money on infrastructure. It is simply their way of telling you they like to make a certain amount of money per client and you are not "it" for them. What happens if your company never reaches their thresholds? Fee-gouging goes on indefinitely and the plan provider ends up right where they wanted to be on profit anyway. Do not go for this. Any business can get ultra-low pricing on retirement plans whether you have five employees or 50,000.

Dirty Little Secret #3 - Revenue Sharing

Revenue sharing is a process whereby money gets shared behind the scenes among the service providers to your plan. Revenue sharing is a dead giveaway that you are being steered into high-cost investments and high administrative fees. They take more money from you than is needed so they can have money to pass around. This makes for cozy relationships among companies who refer themselves back and forth and use your money to prop each other up in business.

Dirty Little Secret #4 - High-Cost Plans with Low-Cost Names

Providers are not unwise to the notion that you might ask them to prove you are getting a good deal. One way they overcome this is by stocking your plan with low-cost investment names. Will it surprise you to know that the ultra-high-cost plan you will read about next in "Let's Tackle The Fees" was stocked with an entire lineup of low-cost target-date funds and three index funds? The target-date mutual fund expense ratio is just 0.16%. The index funds charge even less. So how did they get the client to make the leap from their low-cost mindset to agreeing to pay 3.03% in total participant fees? They took the one thing the business owner knew something about and used it against them.

Dirty Little Secret #5 - Share Class Manipulation

This is the equivalent of being charged for premium gasoline at the pump and having regular gas pumped into your vehicle. Share classes are the price tags on mutual funds. There are various share classes of each company's mutual funds, each designed for a specific investor application. When a retirement plan provider puts you in a high-cost share class and gambles you won't notice, they do it so they can collect remuneration from the mutual fund company on top of the other money they already collect from you. This practice is often a dirty side-component to revenue sharing. The chances of you noticing or even comprehending what they are doing to you are EXTREMELY low.

Retirement plans should always use the lowest-cost share class available. The lowest-cost share class at any mutual fund company pays only for the investment management services of the mutual fund company. This means that no remuneration passes from the mutual fund company to the retirement plan provider. All other fees to your plan should then be itemized and attributed to the service provider receiving them. The result will be a transparent and truthful pricing structure. This is how the first fee illustration coming up in "Let's Tackle The Fees" is designed.

Dirty Little Secret #6 - Overpriced Advice

Investment advice services are being offered as an option inside many 401(k), 403(b) and 457(b) plans. This is mostly referred to as a "Managed Account" service. This can be a good thing for people who do not have the confidence to select their own investments, but not if the price is too high. I have seen advice offered for as high as 1% of your account value. Example #2 coming up in "Let's Tackle The Fees" offers advice for 0.60%. The advice is typically being generated by a computer based on a few simple questions you answer. If your account value is $200,000, is that computer-generated advice worth $2,000/yr.? How about $1,200/yr.?

A simple risk-tolerance questionnaire will suffice to get most people invested properly, and then follow my principles of Time, Money and Consistency. You will get to where you need to go. If you want the comfort of having someone advise you within your plan, an appropriately-priced service costs $79/yr. See **401k Optimizer** in "Additional Resources."

Dirty Little Secret #7 - The Long Game

What do you get when you take a bunch of powerful, well-lobbied retirement plan companies with teams of lawyers who stretch from here to the moon and pit them against millions of plan participants who are like drops of water in an ocean? You get "The Long Game." It goes like this.

1. Get the clients to pay as much as they will agree to.

2. Collect ridiculous sums of money year after year.

3. Get sued by one out of 100,000 clients.

4. Fight it out for years in court.

5. Write a check only if the court makes you.

6. Have a steak dinner and laugh it off.

7. Repeat.

Here's A Little Secret For You! You can control the game. The biggest mistake that any organization can make is to try and talk sense to a retirement plan company that is gouging them on fees. If their fees are too high, don't waste your time talking. Kick them off your field and invite another company on to your field whose plan fees are more to your liking.

The Long Game works for them only if they know more than you. Take note of the Total Participant Fee for Example #1 in "Let's Tackle The Fees." The Total Participant Fee of 0.65% is a number you should become familiar with, because in the retirement plan industry it is the number by which all other Total Participant Fees are judged.

Let's Tackle The Fees

What is a company retirement plan but a menu of stocks and bonds that you shop from each payday? Your objective is simple. Pay only low or reasonably-low fees for the shopping experience. Less money for them equals more money for you. Some of you reading this are plan participants and some of you are decision-makers for the company's retirement plan. I hope to deliver the information in a way that helps everyone work together in your quest to pay only low fees.

Understanding how a retirement plan is packaged, priced and sold to an employer is crucial for any employer and employee to making smart decisions when selecting a retirement plan vendor. I am going to make it easy for you by showing two examples. The first example is at the ultra-low end of the fee spectrum and the other at the ultra-high end.

Note: Fee structures will vary from provider to provider in two ways. The first is in how the names of the fees are presented. The second is in the number of fees included. I cover this in more detail next chapter. But for now, let's get to our two examples.

EXAMPLE 1:

This is a standard 401(k) offering of ours with ultra-low fees.

A.   Plan Administration - $1,500 yr.

B.   Account Maintenance Fee - $0

C. Mutual Fund Expense Ratio - 0.16%

D. Asset-Based Charge - 0.08%

E. Advisor Fee - 0.41%

F. **Total Fee To The Business - $1,500**

G. **Total Participant Fee - 0.65%**

Explanation of Fees:

A. Plan Administration - fee to the business for third-party administration.

B. Account Maintenance Fee - custodial fee deducted from participant's account as a dollar amount.

C. Mutual Fund Expense Ratio - mutual fund management fee deducted from participant's account as a percentage. (blended average of the funds)

D. Asset-Based Charge - custodial and recordkeeping fee deducted from participant's account as a percentage.

E. Advisor Fee - financial advisor fee deducted from participant's account as a percentage.

F. Total Fee To The Business - total hard dollar cost billed to the employer annually.

G. Total Participant Fee - total percentage debited from participant's account annually.

EXAMPLE 2:

This is a 401(k) plan we just replaced for a business that was paying ultra-high fees. The plan has $1,917,000 in participant assets.

A. Plan Administration - $2,784 yr.

B. Sponsor Account Fee - $750 yr.

C. Account Maintenance Fee - $0

D. Mutual Fund Expense Ratio - 0.28%

E. Asset-Based Charge - 0.90%

F. Separate Account Charge - 1.85%

G. Managed Account Fee - 0.60%

H. Total Fee To The Business - $3,534

I. Total Participant Fee - 3.03% / 3.63%

Explanation of Fees:

A. Plan Administration - fee to the business for third-party administration.

B. Sponsor Account Fee - fee to the business for unspecified services.

C. Account Maintenance Fee - custodial fee deducted from participant's account as a dollar amount.

D. Mutual Fund Expense Ratio - mutual fund management fee deducted from participant's account as a percentage. (blended average of the funds)

E.   Asset-Based Charge - custodial and recordkeeping fee deducted from participant's account as a percentage.

F.   Separate Account Charge - annuity fee deducted from participant's account as a percentage.

H.   Managed Account Fee - an investment advice fee (optional) deducted from participant's accounts as a percentage.

I.   Total Fee To The Business - total hard dollar cost billed to the employer annually.

J.   Total Participant Fee - total percentage debited from participant's account annually.

Comparison Summary:

1. We reduced the participant's fees by 2.38%. The Total Participant Fee dropped from 3.03% to 0.65%.

2. The first-year savings to participants company-wide is $45,624.60. This is money that was being deducted from participant's accounts, which will now stay in the participant's account every year going forward.
    ($1,917,000 x .0238)

3. We cut the fees to the employer by 57.5%.
    ($3,534 – 1500) / $3534

Synopsis:

This company and its employees were experiencing a Category 5 hurricane, but would you believe it used to be worse? This company paid even higher fees when they started the plan because of Dirty Little

Secret #2 - Pricing Thresholds. This plan also is showing you Dirty Little Secret #1 - The Separate Account Charge in action. This insidious fee is crushing the retirement futures of hard-working Americans in every segment of the private and public-sector across all 50 states.

Now, let's see how bad the wind and rain are over at your place.

Let's Tackle Your Fees

Having surveyed hundreds of fee-conscious retirement plan participants, one thing never ceases to amaze me. Almost every one of them never knew they were paying any fees beyond the mutual fund expense ratio. They always felt that if they looked at their statements and saw the usual list of low-cost fund names, then their employer must have them in a good place. They also assumed that the employer vetted a list of 401(k) providers prior to selecting the one they are with. That is usually not the case. In my experience, 99 out of 100 employers went with the first proposal they received. They have no frame of reference for quantifying retirement plan fees and are usually unaware that they may have made a less-than-desirable choice of retirement plan provider.

Assessing your plan's fees is not just a task for company management. It is for anyone reading this book. Every employee at every workplace has the information already available to do a deep dive on your plan's fees. If you spot excessive fees in your plan, take your analysis and this book to the CEO, CFO or HR and let them know. If you want a second opinion to make sure you are calculating things correctly, my contact information is all over this book. As I mentioned at the beginning, the best 401(k), 403(b) and 457(b) plans come about when employees speak their concerns, and everyone pulls together to make your organization's retirement plan the best it can be.

Retirement plan fees break down along two lines; fees paid by the employer and fees paid by participants which are debited from participant accounts. Your objective is to calculate the total fees being debited from participant's accounts and determine if they are ultra-low, reasonably low or "it's time to move our plan to another company."

If you get stuck in this exercise, simply refer to the two examples in "Let's Tackle The Fees" to see how plan services are itemized and calculated.

The benchmark for an ultra-low Total Participant Fee in 401(k), 403(b) and 457(b) plans is 0.65%.

The method for finding 401(k) plan fees varies from that of 403(b) and 457(b) plans.

For 401(k) plans... Total participant fee is comprised of two groupings. The first grouping is the mutual fund expenses. There are usually 10-20 funds or more in a plan and an equal number of mutual fund expense ratios to consider. I will cover how to reduce that down to a single number in more detail below.

The second grouping is the fees of all other service providers to your plan. 401(k) plan fees are reported to the employer on fee disclosure 408(b)(2) and participants on fee disclosure 404(a)(5). The Department of Labor's 404(a)(5) fee transparency efforts are designed to provide participants with at least an annual-and in some cases a quarterly-breakdown of the fees that they are directly incurring for plan administration, investment management and advisor services.

Here is a list of the most common participant fees deducted from participant's 401(k) accounts. Your 404(a)(5) may reference them by slightly different names, and you may even encounter a fee not listed here. Simply track them down and add them up.

- o Account Maintenance Fee – annual custodial fee.

- o Mutual Fund Expense Ratio - mutual fund management fee.

- o Asset-Based Charge - custodial and recordkeeping fee.

- o Separate Account Charge - annuity fee charged in group variable annuity plans.

- o Managed Account Fee - investment advice fee for participants who wish to have their investments selected for them.

- o Advisor Fee - financial advisor fee.

- o 3(16), 3(21) & 3(38) Fee - fiduciary services provider fees.

FYI, a "basis point" is equal to 1/100th of one percent. One hundred basis points is equal to 1%. If you see a fee listed as 15 basis points, it is 0.15% or 15/100th of 1%. Add the basis points of the fees together to arrive at your Total Participant Fee. 198 basis points, for example, equals 1.98%

Calculating Mutual Fund Expense Ratio

The best way to quantify mutual fund expense ratio is to calculate the blended average of the funds in your plan. Simply add the expense ratios of all the funds in your plan and then divide by the number of funds. Do not include money market funds, fixed interest rate funds and cash reserve funds in your calculations. They are not relevant to obtaining a representation of your plan's fund expenses. Not everyone in the plan invests in the same funds, so a blended average will give you a general sense of whether fund lineup is overall reasonably-priced.

Example:

"XYZ Large Company Growth Fund A"	0.98%
"PDQ Small Cap Core Fund R"	0.45%
"LMN International Value Fund A"	1.2%
"JKL Global Investor R"	0.90%
Total	3.53%
Blended Average (3.53% / 4)	0.88%

Now, simply add your mutual fund expense ratio to your fees listed on your 404(a)(5) to obtain your Total Participant Fee. If your plan is by a life insurance company, do not forget to locate the Separate Account Charge. It is likely not disclosed on your 404(a)(5), so scour your enrollment booklet and other documents until you find it. Remember the signs I told you about in Dirty Little Secret #1. If you see the signs, the Separate Account Charge exists. Do not stop looking until you find it.

For 403(b) and 457(b) plans... The process is the same, except you do not receive a 404(a)(5). Your plan's fees will all be listed among the plan website, enrollment guide and your statements.

You are looking for three things; mutual fund expense ratio, separate account charge if your plan is by a life insurance company and an optional managed account fee.

For calculating your mutual fund expense ratio, you will use the same method as above.

For the separate account charge, it will either be added to the mutual fund expense ratio or buried in fine print. I found one company's separate account charge buried on the back of the last page of the participant's statement. The employer had argued with me that it didn't exist. Here is where the fee was not disclosed; in the thick and glossy participant enrollment guide, the plan's website and the participant's online accounts. It is extremely important that you locate that fee. These companies do their best to ensure you won't.

For the managed account fee, you simply need to find it and determine its reasonableness. Refer to Dirty Little Secret #6 - Overpriced Advice to gain perspective on the cost of this fee in your plan, should it exist.

The last chapter of this book contains a glossary of terms to further assist you. This book also comes with phone-a-friend. If you need help calculating your plan's fees, starting up a plan, moving your plan to lower fees or mapping your exit strategy from work to retirement, please do not hesitate to contact me.

Michael J. Marini

Email - mmarini@ksifa.com

Phone - 407 924-7950

LinkedIn - www.linkedin.com/in/michaeljmarini

Website - www.orlando401kspecialists.com

Please leave a book review on Amazon.

Thank you for reading!

Now, for my final thoughts...

Final Thoughts

When I think about the mountain of money being drained out of retirement accounts every year by excessive fees, I think about the negative impact it has on all of us as Americans.

In my area where I live and work there is approximately $2 billion in 401(k), 403(b) and 457(b) plans. By my estimate that makes for approximately $25 million in excessive fees being drained from these workplace retirement accounts. That's $25 million this year, but what happens to the future compounding on the $25 million had it stayed invested in each person's account where it belonged? It is gone forever. And what about next year's $25 million in squandered fees? Well, it is not $25 million next year. It is much more. As the collective balances rise in participant's accounts, so does the amount of fees being drained. The retirement plan providers collecting high fees love this. And they will say whatever it takes to keep you from quitting them. Regardless of what they say, the truth lies within the documents. Dig it out. Become the authority on the fees they are collecting from you.

When these companies systematically drain excessive fees from our retirement accounts it hurts us all. They don't just take money from you and from your heirs. They drain money out of our economy that results in stifled futures and lost jobs. When people have less money to spend there is less consumer demand and less people get employed. Social security checks become more important and we wonder why the middle class falls backward while the wealthy and the corporations move forward.

The retirement plan companies believe they are smarter than you. But they are not smarter than you, nor are they more powerful than you. Your retirement dollars coming from your paycheck are the lifeblood of their existence. They would love to keep fattening up their piggy bank at the expense of your piggy bank. Do not let them. You have the power to take back what belongs to you. Do it! For yourself. For your family. For our country. For Piggy!

Additional Resources

401k Optimizer

401k Optimizer is a service from Howard Capital Management that will recommend which funds to select in your 401(k), 403(b) or 457(b) retirement account. Then it will send you updated recommendations quarterly or whenever a change is suggested to be made. 401k Optimizer works with any retirement plan. The service comes to you independently of your employer, not as an offering of your plan.

401k Optimizer is $79/year. Contact me for group pricing.

For more information visit: https://www.401koptimizer.com

Make sure to select me as your financial adviser.

Internal Revenue Service

The IRS website is the definitive source for employers and employees regarding the types of retirement plans available to each type of business entity, governmental agency and non-profit. You can research features, contribution limits and more.

- Individual Retirement Accounts
- Roth Individual Retirement Accounts
- 401(k) Plans
- 401(a) Plans
- 403(b) Plans

- SIMPLE IRA Plans - Savings Incentive Match Plans for Employees

- SEP Plans - Simplified Employee Plans

- SARSEP Plans - Salary Reduction Simplified Employee Pension

- Payroll Deduction Individual Retirement Accounts

- Profit-Sharing Plans

- Defined Benefit Plans

- Money Purchase Plans

- ESOP Plans - Employee Stock Ownership Plan

- 457 Plans

- 409A Non-Qualified Deferred Compensation Plan

- Help with Choosing a Retirement Plan

For more information visit:

https://www.irs.gov/retirement-plans/plan-sponsor/types-of-retirement-plans

https://www.irs.gov/retirement-plans/plan-participant-employee/retirement-topics

United States Department of Labor

This information is recommended reading for 401(k) plan sponsors (employers). "ERISA Fiduciary Advisor" is the definitive source for information to assist employers in meeting their fiduciary obligations under the law.

Offering a retirement plan can be both rewarding and challenging for an employer. The employees participating in the plan, their beneficiaries, and the employer all benefit from a retirement plan. By deciding to offer the plan, the employer also takes on certain responsibilities and requirements in administering the plan and managing its assets.

Fiduciaries are those individuals and/or entities who manage an employee benefit plan and its assets. Employers often hire outside professionals, sometimes called third-party service providers, or use an internal administrative committee or human resources department to manage some or all of a plan's day-to-day operations. Employers who have hired outside professionals or who use internal committees/resources still have fiduciary responsibilities.

The Employee Retirement Income Security Act (ERISA) is the Federal law that sets standards of conduct for fiduciaries. This Advisor is designed to provide an overview of the basic fiduciary responsibilities applicable to retirement plans under the law. While employees are welcome to review the information in this Advisor, the intended audience is employers and third-party service providers, such as accountants, attorneys, third party administrators, and others directly involved in the plan.

ERISA Fiduciary Advisor answers these important questions.

- o   Who are the plan's fiduciaries?
- o   What are fiduciary responsibilities?

- What are my liabilities as a fiduciary and how can I limit them?
- Are some transactions prohibited? Is there a way to make them permissible?
- What are the fiduciary responsibilities regarding employee
- contributions?
- Is hiring a service provider a fiduciary function, and if so, what do I need to do?
- What should a fiduciary consider regarding fees in deciding on service providers and plan investments.
- When is providing investment advice a fiduciary function?
- How do employees get information about the plan?
- What are the reporting requirements for the plan?
- What help is available for employers who make mistakes in operating a plan?
- Can a fiduciary terminate its duties?
- Understanding fiduciary responsibilities is important for the security of a retirement plan and compliance with the law. The following tips may be a helpful starting point.
- Have you identified your plan fiduciaries and are they clear about the extent of their fiduciary responsibilities?

o   If participants make their own investment decisions have you provided sufficient information for them to exercise control in making those decisions?

o   Are you aware of the schedule to deposit participant's contributions in the plan and have you made sure it complies with the law?

o   If you are hiring third-party service providers have you looked at the number of providers, given each potential provider the same information and considered whether the fees are reasonable for the services provided?

o   Have you documented the hiring process?

o   Are you prepared to monitor your plan's service providers?

o   Have you identified parties-in-interest to the plan and taken steps to monitor transactions with them?

o   Are you aware of the major exemptions under ERISA that permit transactions with parties-in-interest, especially those key for plan operations (such as hiring service providers and making loans to participants.)

o   Have you reviewed your plan document considering current plan operations and made necessary updates? After amending the plan have you provided participants with an updated SPD or SMM?

- o Do the individuals handling plan funds or other property have a fidelity bond?

Visit ERISA Fiduciary Advisor:

https://webapps.dol.gov/elaws/ERISAFiduciary.htm

Employee Benefits Security Administration

The EBSA is an agency of the United States Department of Labor. Here are just a few of the topics that employers and employees can research on the EBSA website.

- o 401(k) plans for small businesses
- o 401(k) plan fee disclosure forms
- o Exemption procedures under federal pension law
- o How to obtain employee benefit documents from DOL
- o Meeting your fiduciary responsibilities
- o Payroll Deduction IRAs for small businesses
- o QDRO - Qualified Domestic Relations Orders
- o Reporting and disclosure guide for employee benefit plans
- o Retirement correction programs
- o SEP retirement plans for small businesses
- o Selecting an auditor for your employee benefit plan
- o Selecting and monitoring pension consultants
- o SIMPLE IRA plans for small businesses
- o Tips for employers with retirement plans

- Tips for selecting and monitoring service providers for your employee benefit plan

- Understanding retirement plan fees and expenses

- A look at 401(k)plan fees

- Filing a claim for your retirement benefits

- New employee savings tips - time is on your side

- Savings fitness - a guide to your money and your financial future

- Taking the mystery out of retirement planning

- Top 10 ways to prepare for retirement

- What you should know about your retirement plan

- Women and retirement savings

Visit the EBSA: https://www.dol.gov/agencies/ebsa

Glossary of Terms

○ 3(16) Fiduciary: The person responsible for day to day operations of the 401(k) plan. Responsibilities include signing and submitting Form 5500, plan document maintenance, participant enrollment responsibilities, distribution of participant notices, overseeing distributions and loans and maintaining a fidelity bond.

○ 3(21) Fiduciary: Anyone who provides investment advice for a fee to a retirement plan.

○ 3(38) Fiduciary: The party exercising discretionary authority over selection of the 401(k) plan's investment lineup.

○ 404(a)(5): A 401(k) participant fee disclosure detailing the charges they are directly incurring for plan administration, investment management and advisor services. Disclosures are delivered to participants at least annually.

○ 408(b)(2): A requirement that covered service providers of ERISA plans provide fiduciaries with a description of the services they provide, the compensation they expect to receive in connection with those services, and identification of any services provided as a fiduciary.

○ 404(c): an optional regulation on plan sponsor to provide certain information and fund choices so plan participants can make informed decisions about their retirement plan investments.

○ 12b-1 Fee: A fee assessed on certain mutual funds or share classes permitted under an SEC rule to help cover the costs associated with marketing and selling the fund. 12b-1 fees may also be used to cover shareholder servicing expenses.

○ Active Management: The trading of securities to take advantage of market opportunities as they occur, in contrast to passive management. Active managers rely on research, market forecasts, and their own judgment and experience in selecting securities to buy and sell.

○ Account Maintenance Fee: Annual fee assessed against participant's retirement accounts for custodial services.

○ Advisory Fee: Fee charged by an Investment Advisor Representative (IAR) for providing advice and service to retirement plans.

○ Aggressive: An investment approach that accepts above-average risk of loss in return for potentially above-average investment returns.

○ Aggressive Growth Fund: An investment fund that takes higher risk of loss in return for potentially higher returns or gains.

○ AMEX Major Market Index (XMI): An index that is an average of 20 Blue Chip Industrial Stocks.

○ Annual Contribution Percentage Test (ACP): A test to determine whether matching contributions and employee after-tax contributions made on behalf of employees discriminate in favor of highly compensated employees. To perform the test, the average contribution percentage for highly compensated employees for a plan year is compared to the average contribution percentage for non-highly compensated employees for the same plan year or for the prior plan year, depending on whether the plan is using the current year testing method or the prior year testing method.

○ Actual Deferral Percentage Test (ADP): A test to determine whether elective deferrals made on behalf of employees discriminate in favor of highly compensated employees. To perform the test, the average deferral percentage for highly compensated employees for a plan year is compared to the average deferral percentage for non-highly compensated employees for the same plan year or for the prior plan year, depending on whether the plan is using the current year testing method or the prior year testing method.

○ Annual Report: A yearly report or record of an investment's (e.g., a mutual fund's or company's) financial position and operations.

○ Annual Rate of Return: The annual rate of gain or loss on an investment expressed as a percentage.

○ Appreciation: An increase in the value of an investment.

○ Asset: Anything with commercial or exchange value owned by a business, institution or individual. Examples include cash, real estate and investments.

- Asset Allocation: A method of investing by which investors include a range of different investment classes such as stocks, bonds, and cash alternatives or equivalents in their portfolios. See Diversification.

- Asset Allocation Fund: A common trust fund or mutual fund that spreads its portfolio among a wide variety of investments, including domestic and foreign stocks and bonds, government securities, and real estate stocks. This gives small investors far more diversification than they could get allocating money on their own. Some of these funds keep the proportions allocated between different sectors relatively constant, while others alter the mix as market conditions change.

- Asset-Based Charge: A charge levied against the assets of a retirement plan expressed as a percentage, such as 0.90%, or 90 Basis Points.

- Asset Class: A group of securities or investments that have similar characteristics and behave similarly in the marketplace. Three common asset classes are equities (e.g., stocks), fixed income (e.g., bonds), and cash alternatives or equivalents (e.g., money market funds).

- Audit: An annual requirement for 401(k) plans with 100 plus participants.

- Automatic Contribution Arrangement: A feature in a plan whereby a covered employee's compensation is reduced by an amount specified in the plan and contributed to the plan on the employee's behalf unless the employee makes an affirmative election to have a different amount or no amount contributed to the plan. In the case of a 401k plan with an automatic contribution arrangement, the amounts withheld from employees' compensation are contributed to the plan as elective deferrals and the percentage of compensation contributed is called the default deferral rate.

- Auto Enrollment: The practice of enrolling all eligible employees in a plan and beginning participant deferrals without requiring the employees to submit a request to participate. Plan design specifies how these automatic deferrals will be invested. Employees who do not want to make deferrals to the plan must actively file a request to be excluded from the plan. Participants can generally change the amount of pay that is deferred and how it is invested.

o Auto Escalation: A plan which automatically increases the percentage of (retirement) funds saved from salary. This type of plan generally features a default or standard contribution escalation rate.

o Average Annual Total Return: The yearly average percentage increase or decrease in an investment's value that includes dividends, gains, and changes in share price.

o Back-end Load: A fee imposed by some funds when shares are redeemed (sold back to the fund) during the first few years of ownership. Also called a contingent deferred sales charge.

o Balanced Fund: A fund with an investment objective of both long-term growth and income, through investment in both stocks and bonds.

o Barclay's Capital U.S. Aggregate Bond Index: A common index widely used to measure performance of U.S. bond funds.

o Base Fee: Annual cost charged to the plan sponsor for third-party administration and recordkeeping services.

o Basic Matching Contribution: A type of safe harbor 401(k) plan contribution. It is a qualified matching contribution equal to the sum of 100% of the participant's elective deferrals that do not exceed 3% of compensation and 50% of the participant's elective deferrals that exceed 3% of compensation but not 5% of compensation.

o Basis Point: One-hundredth of one percent, or 0.01%. For example, 20 basis points equal 0.20%. Investment expenses, interest rates, and yield differences among bonds are often expressed in basis points.

o Benchmark: An unmanaged group of securities whose performance is used as a standard to measure investment performance. Some well-known benchmarks are the Dow Jones Industrial Average and the S&P 500 Index.

o Blackout Notice: Required to be provided to plan participants 30 days before a plan enters the Blackout Period.

o Blackout Period: When a plan sponsor decides to switch from one plan vendor to another, there is typically a period during which participants are not permitted to make changes in their investment selections. This is known as the blackout period. Once the blackout period commences and until it ends, participants can no longer direct the investments in their accounts. Blackout periods can last up to 60 days.

o Bond: A debt security which represents the borrowing of money by a corporation, government, or other entity. The borrowing institution repays the amount of the loan plus a percentage as interest. Income funds generally invest in bonds.

o Bond Fund: A fund that invests primarily in bonds and other debt instruments.

o Bond Rating: A rating or grade that is intended to indicate the credit quality of a bond, considering the financial strength of its issuer and the likelihood that it will repay the debt. Agencies such as Standard & Poor's, Moody's Investors Service, and Fitch issue ratings for different bonds, ranging from AAA (highly unlikely to default) to D (in default).

o Broker: A person who acts as an intermediary between the buyer and seller of a security, insurance product, or mutual fund, often paid by commission. The terms broker, broker/dealer, and dealer are sometimes used interchangeably.

o Brokerage Window: A plan feature that permits participants to purchase investments that are not included among the plan's general menu of designated investment alternatives.

o Bundled Plan: A 401k package which includes all investment, administration, education, and recordkeeping that is sold as one unit. This stands in contrast to a basic 401k plan in which the plan sponsor can individually hire each component provider separately.

o Capitalization (Cap): The total market value of a company's outstanding equity.

o Capital Appreciation Fund: An investment fund that seeks growth in share prices by investing primarily in stocks whose share prices are expected to rise.

o Capital Gain: An increase in the value of an investment, calculated by the difference between the net purchase price and the net sale price.

o Capital Loss: The loss in the value of an investment, calculated by the difference between the purchase price and the net sale price.

o Capital Preservation: An investment goal or objective to keep the original investment amount (the principal) from decreasing in value.

o Cash Alternative or Cash Equivalent: An investment that is short term, highly liquid, and has high credit quality.

o Cash Balance Plan: A type of defined benefit plan that describes a participant's accrued benefit as a hypothetical account balance or a single-sum amount.

o Catch up Provision: A provision found in some 401k plans that allows an eligible employee who are at least age 50 to make higher annual contributions in the years prior to retirement.

o Churning: The unethical and excessive trading of a client account in order to generate commissions for a broker, but which may not in the best interests of the client. Not only does the client pay high commissions, they also get stuck with a high tax bills due to the short-term holding of assets.

o Cliff Vesting: A 401k plan with "Cliff Vesting" vests 100% of employer contributions after a specified number of years of service. After three years of service, benefits must be fully vested.

o Collective Investment Fund: Investments created by a bank or trust company for employee benefit plans, such as 401(k) plans, that pool the assets of retirement plans for investment purposes. They are governed by rules and regulations that apply to banks and trust companies instead of being registered with the SEC. These funds are also referred to as collective or commingled trusts.

o Commission: Compensation paid to a broker or other salesperson for his or her role when investments are bought or sold.

o Common Stock: An investment that represents a share of ownership in a corporation.

○ Company Stock Fund: A fund that invests primarily in employer securities that also maintains a cash position for liquidity purposes.

○ Competing Funds: An investment fund that is identified by the investment manager of another fund and which is subject to special rules relating to an investor's ability to buy and sell investments between the two funds. See Equity Wash Restriction.

○ Compliance Testing: Testing required by the IRS to make sure that the 401k plan is fair to both highly compensated and ordinary employees.

○ Compounding: The cumulative effect that reinvesting an investment's earnings can have by generating additional earnings of their own.

○ Conservative: An investment approach that accepts lower rewards in return for potentially lower risks.

○ Contingent Beneficiary: A contingent beneficiary stands second-in-line, behind the primary beneficiary, to inherit the assets of a retirement plan.

○ Contingent Deferred Sales Charge (CDSC): A fee imposed when shares of a mutual fund or a variable annuity contract are redeemed (sold) during the first few years of ownership. Also called a back-end load.

○ Corporate Bond: A bond issued by a corporation, rather than by a government. The credit risk for a corporate bond is based on the re-payment ability of the company that issued the bond.

○ Corrective Distribution: A distribution of funds from the plan to correct a nondiscrimination test or to correct a contribution in excess of a statutory limitation.

○ Credit Risk: The risk that a bond issuer will default, meaning not repay principal or interest to the investor as promised. Credit risk is also known as "default risk."

○ Current Yield: The current rate of return of an investment calculated by dividing its expected income payments by its current market price.

- Custodian: A person or entity (e.g., bank, trust company, or other organization) responsible for holding financial assets.

- Defined Benefit Plan: A plan under which each participant's benefits are not held in separate accounts, but instead, a formula stated in the plan provides for determinable accrued benefits.

- Defined Contribution Plan: A plan which provides for an individual account for each participant. Benefits are based on the amount contributed to the participant's account, and any income, expenses, gains and losses, and any forfeitures of accounts of other participants which may be allocated to such participant's account.

- Default Deferral Rate: In the case of an automatic contribution arrangement in a 401(k) plan, the percentage of compensation, specified in the plan, withheld automatically from a covered participant's compensation (unless the participant elects otherwise) and contributed to the plan as an elective deferral.

- Deflation: The opposite of inflation – a decline in the prices of goods and services.

- Depreciation: A decrease in the value of an investment.

- Designated Investment Alternative: The investment options picked by your plan into which participants can direct the investment of their plan accounts.

- Designated Roth Contribution: An elective deferral designated as a Roth contribution when contributed to the plan and which is not excludable from gross income.

- Determination Letter: A written statement issued by the Internal Revenue Service to an employer as to the acceptability of the form of a specific plan and any related trust or custodial account satisfying the tax-qualification requirements under §401(a) and related sections.

- Direct Rollover: A rollover made from one plan to another plan without being distributed to the participant.

o Discretionary Match: A matching contribution permitted under the terms of the plan but not required. The plan sponsor can choose whether to make a discretionary match on a year-by-year basis. The plan sponsor can also choose the amount of the match that will be made.

o Discrimination Testing: All tax qualified retirement plans must be administered in compliance with several regulations to meet Internal Revenue Service guidelines, every tax qualified retirement plan (like a 401k) must pass a series of numerical measurements each year. These include the ADP Test (Actual Deferral Percentage), ACP Test (Actual Contribution Percentage), Multiple Use Test and Top-heavy Test. Typically, doing these tests is called discrimination testing.

o Distributions and Withdrawals: When money is withdrawn from a 401k plan, the withdrawal is referred to as a distribution. 401k plan assets can be withdrawn without penalty after age 59 1/2. Employees are required to begin taking distributions after age 70 1/2.

o Diversification: The practice of investing in multiple asset classes and securities with different risk characteristics to reduce the risk of owning any single investment.

o Dividend: Money an investment fund or company pays to its stockholders, typically from profits. The amount is usually expressed on a per-share basis.

o Dollar Cost Averaging: A process of buying securities at regular intervals and at a fixed dollar amount. When prices are lower, the investor buys more shares or units; when prices are higher, the investor purchases fewer shares or units. Over time, this typically results in a better average price for all shares or units purchased.

o Dow Jones Industrial Average (Dow or DJIA): A widely followed price-weighted index of 30 of the largest, most widely held U.S. stocks.

o Elective Deferral: An amount elected by a participant to be contributed to a plan, thereby deferring the receipt of the cash as income. Elective deferrals can be either pre-tax elective deferrals or designated Roth contributions.

○ Emerging Market: Generally, economies that are in the process of growth and industrialization, such as in Africa, Asia, Eastern Europe, the Far East, Latin America, and the Middle East which, while relatively undeveloped, may hold significant growth potential in the future. Investing in these economies may provide significant rewards, and significant risks. May also be called developing markets.

○ Emerging Market Fund: A fund that invests primarily in emerging market countries.

○ Employer Securities: Securities issued by an employer of employees covered by a retirement plan that may be used as a plan investment option.

Employer Matching Contribution: The amount, if any, that the employer contributes to the employee's 401k account. Matching contributions are usually configured to provide a set percentage of an employee's contribution up to a fixed limit.

○ Employer Discretionary Contribution: Some employers also make an additional contribution at plan-year end in the form of increased matching contributions and/or a profit sharing contribution. These employer contributions are considered a tax-deductible business expense and also grow on a tax-deferred basis.

○ Enhanced Matching Contribution: A matching contribution under a safe harbor 401k plan that provides each participant with a matching contribution that is greater than the basic matching contribution.

○ Enrollment Package: For some plans, employees must enroll to participate. To enroll, a participant may be required to complete printed forms, or the plan may allow enrollment over the phone or online. The enrollment package generally contains documents that describe the plan and instructions for proper enrollment in the plan.

○ Equity/Equities: A security or investment representing ownership in a corporation, unlike a bond, which represents a loan to a borrower. Often used interchangeably with "stock."

○ Equity Fund: A fund that invests primarily in equities.

o Equity Wash Restriction: A provision in certain stable value or fixed income products under which transfers made from the stable value or fixed income product are required to be directed to an equity fund or other non-competing investment option of the plan for a stated period of time (usually 90 days) before those funds may be invested in any other plan-provided competing fixed income fund (such as a money market fund).

o Exchange Traded Fund (ETF): An investment company, such as a mutual fund, whose shares are traded throughout the day on stock exchanges at market-determined prices.

o Expense Ratio: A measure of what it costs to operate an investment, expressed as a percentage of its assets or in basis points. These are costs the investor pays through a reduction in the investment's rate of return. See Operating Expenses and Total Annual Operating Expenses.

o ERISA: The Employee Retirement Income Security Act of 1974 (ERISA) sets certain standards for 401(k) plan administrators and requires uniform rights for plan participants.

o Federal Deposit Insurance Corporation (FDIC): A federal agency that insures money on deposit in member banks and thrift institutions.

o Fidelity Bond: A fidelity bond, required under section 412 of ERISA specifically insures a plan against losses due to fraud or dishonesty (e.g., theft) on the part of persons (including, but not limited to, plan fiduciaries) who handle plan funds or other property.

o Fiduciary: An individual or a institution charged with the duty of acting for the benefit of another party as to matters coming within the scope of the relationship between them. For example, any person who exercises any discretionary authority or control over the management of a 401k retirement plan or its assets. A fiduciary is to act solely in the interest of plan participants and their beneficiaries.

o Financial Industry Regulatory Authority (FINRA): A self-regulatory organization for brokerage firms doing business in the United States. FINRA operates under the supervision of the SEC. The organization's objectives are to protect investors and ensure market integrity.

○ Financial Statements: The written record of the financial status of a fund or company, usually published in the annual report. The financial statements generally include a balance sheet, income statement, and other financial statements and disclosures.

○ FINRA Broker Check: A resource for learning about the professional background, registration/license status and conduct of brokerage firms, individual brokers, investment advisers and firms. If your 401(k) plan has a brokerage window, or if you roll your 401(k) into an IRA at a brokerage firm, you'll want to use FBC to check out the firm and its brokers.

○ Fixed Income Fund: A fund that invests primarily in bonds and other fixed-income securities, often to provide shareholders with current income.

○ Fixed Return Investment: An investment that provides a specific rate of return to the investor.

○ Form 5500: 401(k) return required to be filed annually with the IRS. Form 5500 is public record and can be viewed at the United States Department of Labor website.

○ Front-end Load: A sales charge on mutual funds or annuities assessed at the time of purchase to cover selling costs.

○ Frozen Plan: A plan under which accruals and/or contributions have ceased but assets are still held for participants and beneficiaries.

○ Fund Family: A group or "complex" of mutual funds, each typically with its own investment objective, and managed and distributed by the same company. A Fund Family also could refer to a group of collective investment funds or a group of separate accounts managed and distributed by the same company.

○ Fund of Funds: A mutual fund, collective investment fund or other pooled investment that invests primarily in other mutual funds, collective investment funds or pooled investments rather than investing directly in individual securities (such as stocks, bonds or money market securities).

○ Glide Path: The change over time in a target date fund's asset allocation mix to shift from a focus on growth to a focus on income.

o Global Fund: A fund that invests primarily in securities anywhere in the world, including the United States.

o Government Securities: Any debt obligation issued by a government or its agencies (e.g., Treasury Bills issued by the United States).

o Graded Vesting: The process by which employees gain a certain percentage of irrevocable rights over employer contributions made to the employee's retirement plan account each year until the employee is fully vested.

o Growth Fund: A fund that invests primarily in the stocks of companies with above-average risk in return for potentially above-average gains. These companies often pay small or no dividends and their stock prices tend to have the most ups and downs from day to day.

o Growth and Income Fund: A fund that has a dual strategy of growth or capital appreciation and current income generation through dividends or interest payments.

o Hardship Distribution: An in-service distribution from the plan which is made because the participant has suffered severe financial difficulty, or an extraordinary event as defined by the plan document. To make hardship distributions from a plan, the plan must provide for such distributions.

o Highly-Compensated Employee: Highly compensated employees are people who earned more from their employer, or own a larger stake in the company, than the floor the government has established for this category of worker. The drawback of being highly compensated is that you may be restricted on what you can contribute to a 401(k).

o Inception Date: The date that a fund began operations.

o Income Fund: A fund that primarily seeks current income rather than capital appreciation.

o Index: A benchmark against which to evaluate a fund's performance. The most common indexes for stock funds are the Dow Jones Industrial Average and the Standard & Poor's 500 Index.

o Index Fund: An investment fund that seeks to parallel the performance of a particular stock market or bond market index. Index funds are often referred to as passively managed investments.

o Individual Retirement Account: A personal, tax-sheltered retirement account available to wage earners not covered by a company retirement plan or, if covered, meet certain income limitations.

o IRA Rollover: A provision in the IRA law allowing individuals who receive lump-sum payments from pension or profit-sharing plans to "roll-over" into, or invest that sum in, an IRA.

o In-service Withdrawal: A withdrawal from a retirement savings plan by a participant who remains employed. In-service withdrawals are severely restricted by law and most plans.

o Inflation: The overall general upward price movement of goods and services in an economy. Inflation is one of the major risks to investors over the long term because it erodes the purchasing power of their savings.

o Interest/Interest Rate: The fee charged by a lender to a borrower, usually expressed as an annual percentage of the principal. For example, someone investing in bonds will receive interest payments from the bond's issuer.

o Interest Rate Risk: The possibility that a bond's or bond fund's market value will decrease due to rising interest rates. When interest rates (and bond yields) go up, bond prices usually go down and vice versa.

o International Fund: A fund that invests primarily in the securities of companies located, or with revenues derived from, outside of the United States.

o Investment Adviser: A person or organization hired by an investment fund or an individual to give professional advice on investments and asset management practices.

o Investment Company: A corporation or trust that invests pooled shareholder dollars in securities appropriate to the organization's objective. The most common type of investment company, commonly called a mutual fund, stands ready to buy back its shares at their current net asset value.

○ Investment Objective: The goal that an investment fund or investor seeks to achieve (e.g., growth or income).

○ Investment Return: The gain or loss on an investment over a certain period, expressed as a percentage. Income and capital gains or losses are included in calculating the investment return.

○ Investment Risk: The possibility of losing some or all of the amounts invested or not gaining value in an investment.

○ Key Employee: An employee who at any time during the plan year is meets certain income or ownership criteria.

○ Large Capitalization (Cap): A reference to either a large company stock or an investment fund that invests in the stocks of large companies.

○ Large Cap Fund: A fund that invests primarily in large cap stocks.

○ Large Cap Stocks: Stocks of companies with a large market capitalization. Large caps tend to be well-established companies, so their stocks typically entail less risk than smaller caps, but large-caps also offer less potential for dramatic growth.

○ Lifecycle Fund: A fund designed to provide varying degrees of long-term appreciation and capital preservation based on an investor's age or target retirement date through a mix of asset classes. The mix changes over time to become less focused on growth and more focused on income. Also known as "target date retirement" or "age-based" funds.

○ Lifestyle Fund: A fund that maintains a predetermined risk level and generally uses words such as "conservative," "moderate," or "aggressive" in its name to indicate the fund's risk level. Used interchangeably with "target risk fund."

○ Lipper: A leading mutual fund research and tracking firm. Lipper categorizes funds by objective and size, and then ranks fund performance within those categories.

○ Liquidity: The ease with which an investment can be converted into cash. If a security is very liquid, it can be bought or sold easily. If a security is not liquid, it may take additional time and/or a lower price to sell it.

o Load: A sales charge assessed on certain investments to cover selling costs. A front-end load is charged at the time of purchase. A back-end load is charged at the time of sale or redemption.

o Lump Sum Distribution: A lump-sum distribution is a one-time payout of assets in an account, typically a retirement savings account. When you retire or change jobs, you can take a lump-sum distribution as cash, or you can roll over the distribution into an individual retirement account (IRA). If you take the cash, you owe income tax on the full amount of the distribution, and you may owe an additional 10 percent penalty if you're younger than 59½. If you roll over the lump sum into an IRA, the full amount continues to be tax deferred, and you can postpone paying income tax until you withdraw from the account.

o MSCI EAFE Index: An index known by an acronym for the Europe, Australasia, and Far East markets produced by Morgan Stanley Capital International (MSCI). Markets are represented in the index according to their approximate share of world market capitalization. The index is a widely used benchmark for managers of international stock fund portfolios.

o MSCI World Index: An index of major world stock markets, including the United States. The index is a widely used benchmark for managers of global stock fund portfolios.

o Managed Account: A managed account is a portfolio of stocks or bonds owned by an individual investor. The account has a professional investment manager who makes buy and sell decisions, sometimes in response to the account owner's instructions. Each managed account has an investment objective, and each manager oversees multiple individual accounts invested to meet the same objective.

o Management Fee: A fee or charge paid to an investment manager for its services.

o Market Capitalization or Market Cap: The market value of a company. Market capitalization can be determined by multiplying the number of outstanding shares of a company's stock by the stock's current market price per share.

o Market Risk: The possibility that the value of an investment will fall because of a general decline in the financial markets.

o Matching Contribution: Employer contributions that are made on account of elective deferrals or employee after-tax contributions.

o Maturity Date: The date on which the principal amount of a loan, bond, or any other debt becomes due and is to be paid in full.

o Mid Capitalization (Cap): A reference to either a medium sized company stock or an investment fund that invests in the stocks of medium-sized companies.

o Mid Cap Fund: A fund that invests primarily in mid-cap stocks.

o Mid Cap Stocks: Stocks of companies with a medium market capitalization. Mid-caps are often considered to offer more growth potential than larger caps (but less than small caps) and less risk than small caps (but more than large caps).

o Money Market Fund: A mutual fund that invests in short-term, high-grade fixed-income securities, and seeks the highest level of income consistent with preservation of capital (i.e., maintaining a stable share price).

o Morningstar: A leading mutual fund research and tracking firm. Morningstar categorizes funds by objective and size, and then ranks fund performance within those categories.

o Mortality & Expense Charge (M&E): A charge in a qualified retirement plan that is attributed to the underlying annuity product, expressed as a percentage of the participant's assets.

o Multiple Employer Plan (MEP): A plan sponsored by two or more employers where at least two of the sponsoring employers are not members of the same controlled group.

o Mutual Fund: An investment company registered with the SEC that buys a portfolio of securities selected by a professional investment adviser to meet a specified financial goal (investment objective). Mutual funds can have actively managed portfolios, where a professional investment adviser creates a unique mix of investments to meet a particular investment objective, or passively managed portfolios, in which the adviser seeks to parallel the performance of a selected benchmark or index.

○ Mutual Fund Expense Ratio: A measure of what it costs to operate an investment, expressed as a percentage of its assets or in basis points. These are costs the investor pays through a reduction in the investment's rate of return. See Operating Expenses and Total Annual Operating Expenses.

○ Named Fiduciary: The plan document must name one or more fiduciaries (called the "Named Fiduciary") with the duty and the power under ERISA to control, manage and administer the plan. The Named Fiduciary can be an employee of the plan sponsor or an independent party.

○ NASDAQ: The National Association of Securities Dealers Automated Quotation, also called the "electronic stock market." The NASDAQ composite index measures the performance of more than 5,000 U.S. and non-U.S. companies traded "over the counter" through NASDAQ.

○ Net Asset Value (NAV): The net dollar value of a single investment fund share or unit that is calculated by the fund on a daily basis.

○ New York Stock Exchange (NYSE): The oldest and largest stock exchange in the United States, founded in 1792.

○ No-Load Fund: A mutual fund whose shares are sold without a sales commission and which does not charge a combined 12b-1 fee and service fee of more than 25 basis points or 0.25% per year.

○ Non-Discrimination Rules: Rules denying an employer, employee or both the benefit of tax advantages if the plan discriminates in favor of highly compensated or key employees as demonstrated by government-specified tests.

○ Non-Elective Contribution: An employer contribution to a qualified plan that is neither an elective deferral nor a matching contribution (e.g., a discretionary profit-sharing contribution).

○ Non-Qualified Deferred Compensation Plan: A plan subject to tax, in which the assets of certain employees (usually Highly Compensated Employees) are deferred. These funds may be reached by an employer's creditors.

○ Non-Qualified Plan: A pension plan that does not meet the requirements for preferential tax treatment. This type of plan allows an employer more flexibility and freedom with coverage requirements, benefit structures, and financing methods.

○ Operating Expenses: The expenses associated with running or operating an investment fund. Operating expenses may include custody fees, management fees, and transfer agent fees. See Expense Ratio and Total Annual Operating Expenses.

○ Participant: An employee who is eligible to either make contributions to the Plan or to share in employer contributions to the Plan.

○ Participant Contributions: The dollars that employees contribute to their 401k plans.

○ Participant Directed Account: A plan that allows participants to select their own investment options.

○ Participant Directed Investing: The employee decides how to invest his or her funds. It is the company's responsibility to offer a variety of investment opportunities so that the employee can make investments according to his or her long-term goals and risk.

○ Passive Management: The process or approach to operating or managing a fund in a passive or non-active manner, typically with the goal of mirroring an index. These funds are often referred to as index funds and differ from investment funds that are actively managed.

○ Plan Administrator: The individual, group or corporation named in the plan document as responsible for day to day operations. The plan sponsor is generally the plan administrator if no other entity is named.

○ Plan Document: A written instrument under which the plan is established and operated.

○ Plan Fiduciary: Anyone who exercises discretionary authority or discretionary control over management or administration of the plan, exercises any authority or control over management or disposition of plan assets, or gives investment advice for a fee or other compensation with respect to assets of the plan.

O Plan Provider: A 401(k) plan provider is the mutual fund company, insurance company, brokerage firm or other financial services company that creates and sells the plan your employer selects.

O Plan Sponsor: A 401(k) plan sponsor is an employer who offers the plan to employees. The sponsor is responsible for choosing the plan, the plan provider and the plan administrator, and for deciding which investments will be offered through the plan.

O Plan Trustee: The person who has exclusive authority and discretion to manage and control the assets of the plan; named as such either in the trust document or appointed to the position.

O Plan Year: The calendar or fiscal year for which plan records are maintained.

O Portable: A portable retirement plan is one where you can take your contributions plus any earnings with you when you change jobs. 401(k) plans are portable, and you can usually leave the money with your former employer, roll over the money into your new employer's plan, roll over the money into an IRA or take the cash value of your contributions and any earnings.

O Portfolio: A collection of investments such as stocks and bonds that are owned by an individual, organization, or investment fund.

O Portfolio Manager: The individual, team or firm who makes the investment decisions for an investment fund, including the selection of the individual investments.

O Portfolio Turnover Rate: A measure of how frequently investments are bought and sold within an investment fund during a year. The portfolio turnover rate is usually expressed as a percentage of the total value of an investment fund.

O Principal: The original dollar amount of an investment. Principal may also be used to refer to the face value or original amount of a bond.

- Profit-Sharing Plan: A defined contribution plan that provides a definite predetermined formula for allocating the contributions made to the plan among the participants and for distributing the funds after a fixed number of years, the attainment of a stated age, or upon the prior occurrence of some event such as layoff, illness, disability, retirement, death, or severance from employment.

- Prospectus: The official document that describes certain investments, such as mutual funds, to prospective investors. The prospectus contains information required by the SEC, such as investment objectives and policies, risks, services, and fees.

- Qualified Default Investment Alternative (QDIA): An investment option a plan sponsor may use for 401k plan contributions in the absence of direction from a plan participant.

- Qualified Domestic Relations Order: A judgment, decree or order that creates or recognizes an alternate payee's (such as former spouse, child, etc.) right to receive all or a portion of a participant's retirement plan benefits.

- Qualified Plan: A private retirement plan that meets the rules and regulations of the Internal Revenue Service. Contributions to such a plan are generally tax-deductible; earnings on such contributions are always tax sheltered until withdrawal.

- Rate of Return: The gain or loss on an investment over a period of time. The rate of return is typically reported on an annual basis and expressed as a percentage.

- Real Rate of Return: The rate of return on an investment adjusted for inflation.

- Rebalance: The process of moving money from one type of investment to another to maintain a desired asset allocation.

- Recordkeeper: Maintains participant records and provides the technology platform with which participants may view balances and allocations and conduct plan transactions.

- Redemption: To sell fund shares back to the fund. Redemption can also be used to mean the repayment of a bond on or before the agreed upon pay-off date.

○ Redemption Fee: A fee, generally charged by a mutual fund, to discourage certain trading practices by investors, such as short-term or excessive trading. If a redemption fee is charged it is done when the investment is redeemed or sold.

○ Return: The gain or loss on an investment. A positive return indicates a gain, and a negative return indicates a loss.

○ Risk: The potential for investors to lose some or all the amounts invested or to fail to achieve their investment objectives.

○ Risk Tolerance: An investor's ability and willingness to lose some or all of an investment in exchange for greater potential returns.

○ Rollover: The transfer of a qualified plan distribution from one qualified plan or individual retirement arrangement to another qualified plan or individual retirement arrangement

○ Roth 401(k): A 401k feature that allows employees to make elective contributions on an after-tax basis. Withdrawals, generally after age 59½, of any money from the account (including investment gains) are tax-free.

○ Roth Contribution: An elective deferral designated as a Roth contribution when contributed to the plan and which is not excludable from gross income.

○ Round Trip Restriction: A policy that limits the number of times an investor can exchange into and out of a fund within a given time frame. This is intended to discourage frequent trading that increases the costs to all the fund's investors.

○ Russell Indexes: A group of indexes that are widely used to benchmark investment performance. The most common Russell index is the Russell 2000 Index, an index of U.S. small cap stocks, which measures the performance of the 2,000 smallest U.S. companies in the Russell 3000 Index.

○ Safe Harbor 401(k): A type of 401(k) plan that is exempt from the ADP test and the ACP test and not subject to the top-heavy rules. The plan must meet certain notice and employer contribution requirements. The employer must make either a safe harbor non-elective contribution or a qualified matching contribution that is either a basic matching contribution or an enhanced matching contribution. For purposes of this questionnaire, a safe harbor 401(k) plan does not include a QACA or a SIMPLE 401(k) plan.

○ Safe Harbor Non-Elective Contribution: A type of safe harbor 401(k) plan contribution. It is a qualified non-elective contribution equal to 3% of a participant's compensation.

○ Sales Charge: A charge for buying an investment.

○ Sector Fund: A fund that invests in a particular or specialized segment of the marketplace, such as stocks of companies in the software, healthcare, or real estate industries.

○ Securities and Exchange Commission (SEC): Government agency created by Congress in 1934 to regulate the securities industry and to help protect investors. The SEC is responsible for ensuring that the securities markets operate fairly and honestly.

○ Security: A general term for stocks, bonds, mutual funds, and other investments.

○ Separate Account: An insurance company account that is segregated or separate from the insurance company's general assets. Also refers to a fund managed by an investment adviser for a single plan.

○ Separate Account Charge: A charge in a qualified retirement plan that is attributed to the underlying annuity product, expressed as a percentage of the participant's assets.

○ Service Provider: A company that provides some type of service to a 401k plan, including managing assets, recordkeeping, providing plan education, and plan administration.

○ Share: A representation of ownership in a company or investment fund.

o Share Class: Some investment funds and companies offer more than one type or group of shares, each of which is considered a class (e.g., "Class A," "Advisor" or "Institutional" shares). For most investment funds each class has different fees and expenses, but all of the classes invest in the same pool of securities and share the same investment objectives.

o Shareholder: An owner of shares in an investment fund or corporation.

o Shareholder-Type Fees: Any fee charged against your investment for purchase and sale, other than the total annual operating expenses.

o Small Capitalization (Cap): A reference to either a small company stock or an investment fund that invests in the stocks of small companies.

o Small Cap Fund: A fund that invests primarily in small-cap stocks.

o Small Cap Stocks: Stocks of companies with a smaller market capitalization. Small caps are often considered to offer more growth potential than large caps and mid caps but with more risk.

o Socially Responsible Investing (SRI): An investments strategy that only purchases securities of individual companies that espouse some form of social responsibility, e.g., "green" funds that target investments reflecting environmental awareness.

o Sponsor Account Fee: Fee charged to the business for unspecified plan services.

o Stable Value Fund: An investment fund that seeks to preserve principal, provide consistent returns and liquidity. Stable value funds include collective investment funds sponsored by banks or trust companies or contracts issued by insurance companies.

o Standard & Poor's 500 Stock Index (S&P 500): An index comprised of 500 widely held common stocks considered to be representative of the U.S. stock market in general. The S&P 500 is often used as a benchmark for equity fund performance.

o Stock: A security that represents an ownership interest in a corporation.

○ Stock Fund: A fund that invests primarily in stocks.

○ Stock Symbol: An abbreviation using letters and numbers assigned to securities to identify them. Also see Ticker Symbol.

○ Summary Plan Description (SPD): The summary plan description describes, in plain language, the provisions of the plan and the participant's benefits and rights under the plan.

○ Summary Prospectus: A short-form prospectus that mutual funds generally may use with investors if they make the long-form prospectus and additional information available online or on paper upon request.

○ Target Date Fund: A fund designed to provide varying degrees of long-term appreciation and capital preservation based on an investor's age or target retirement date through a mix of asset classes. The mix changes over time to become less focused on growth and more focused on income. Also known as a "lifecycle fund."

○ Target Risk Fund: A fund that maintains a predetermined asset mix and generally uses words such as "conservative," "moderate," or "aggressive" in its name to indicate the fund's risk level. Often used interchangeably with "lifestyle fund."

○ Tax-Free Rollover: Provision whereby an individual receiving a lump sum distribution from a qualified pension or profit sharing plan can preserve the tax deferred status of these funds by a "rollover" into an IRA or another qualified plan if rolled over within sixty days of receipt.

○ Third-Party Administrator: A party hired by a plan or its fiduciaries to aid in performing management and/or recordkeeping functions on behalf of the plan.

○ Ticker Symbol: An abbreviation using letters and numbers assigned to securities and indexes to identify them. Also see Stock Symbol.

○ Time Horizon: The amount of time that an investor expects to hold an investment before taking money out.

o Total Annual Operating Expenses: A measure of what it costs to operate an investment, expressed as a percentage of its assets, as a dollar amount, or in basis points. These are costs the investor pays through a reduction in the investment's rate of return. See Expense Ratio and Operating Expenses.

o Trust Company / Trustee: A person or entity (e.g., bank, trust company, or other organization) that is responsible for the holding and safekeeping of participant's assets. A trustee may also have other duties such as investment management. A trustee that is a "directed trustee" is responsible for the safekeeping of trust assets but has no discretionary investment management duties or authority over the assets.

o Unit: A representation of ownership in an investment that does not issue shares. Most collective investment funds are divided into units instead of shares. See Share.

o Unitholder: An owner of units in an investment. See Shareholder.

o Unit Class: Investment funds that are divided into units (e.g., collective investment funds) instead of shares may offer more than one type or group of units, each of which is considered a class (e.g., "Class A"). For most investment funds, each class has different fees and expenses, but all of the classes invest in the same pool of securities and share the same investment objectives.

o Unit Value: The dollar value of each unit on a given date.

o U.S. Treasury Securities: Debt securities issued by the United States government and secured by its full faith and credit. Treasury securities are the debt financing instruments of the United States Federal government, and they are often referred to simply as Treasuries.

o Value Fund: A fund that invests primarily in stocks that are believed to be priced below what they are worth.

o Variable Account Charge: A charge in a qualified retirement plan that is attributed to the underlying annuity product, expressed as a percentage of the participant's assets.

○ Variable Return Investment: Investments for which the return is not fixed. This term includes stock and bond funds as well as investments that seek to preserve principal but do not guarantee a particular return, e.g., money market funds and stable value funds.

○ Vesting: The period an employee must work at a firm before gaining access to employer-contributed pension income. For 401k plans, employee contributions are immediately vested, but employer contributions may be vested over a period of several years.

○ Vesting Schedule: The schedule in your 401(k) plan that determines when you become vested in the employer's contributions to your account.

○ Volatility: The amount and frequency of fluctuations in the price of a security, commodity, or a market within a specified period. Generally, an investment with high volatility is said to have higher risk since there is an increased chance that the price of the security will have fallen when an investor wants to sell.

○ Wrap Fee: A fee or expense that is added to or "wrapped around" an investment to pay for one or more product features or services.

○ Yield: The value of interest or dividend payments from an investment, usually stated as a percentage of the investment price.

Michael J. Marini

ORLANDO
401k Specialists

NOTES

NOTES

NOTES

NOTES